Good Grief

Poems By
April Bulmer

Copyright © 2023 by April Bulmer

All rights reserved

No part of this book may be reproduced, stored in a retrieval system, or transmitted by any means, electronic, mechanical, photocopying, recording, or otherwise, without written permission from the author or publisher. There is one exception. Brief passages may be quoted in articles or reviews.

ISBN 978-1-55483-542-3

I am grateful to the Ontario Arts Council for their generous funding through their Recommender Grants for Writers program. Special thanks to *Exile, The Literary Quarterly*, *Hamilton Arts & Letters* and Brick Books who recommended me for these grants.

Versions of the poems in this book appeared in the following publications: *Transition, Devour: Art & Lit Canada Summer 2019* and *Stones Beneath the Surface*.

The photo on the front cover was purchased from 123RF. It is called "A Snail Sits on a Dry Plant and in the Rays of the Setting Sun." It was taken by dedalukas. The photo on the back cover was also purchased from 123RF.com. It is called "Beautiful Woman Enjoying Sunset." It was taken by efired.

Introduction

Theodora Hart is a prairie woman, a spiritual soul. She narrates stories of her life in Saskatchewan. First, we learn that she is an abused child who appeals to Jesus and the forces of nature for comfort. Later, she relays her dating experiences with Benny who breaks her heart. Ultimately, she marries the Anglican minister, Father Christopher Hart, who runs her parish. She bares twins, but her daughter dies young. Her mother and husband also pass into the spirit world. She celebrates her devotion to them at her son's wedding.

Theodora speaks in many tongues: In the languages of lean land and of love.

In the moons of her youth,
my mother's womb
is red and firm as the apple
though it sheds like the serpent
a coil of red skin.

She kneels among a sacrifice
of flowers and lifts a bloom:
A chalice to her lips.

But woman's wound does not cease
its ache and blood.
Eve's issue flows between her hips.

Soft earth opens like a woman.
Bulbs crown from her thighs
and bloom.

Fish swim from the river's hips.

But Mama is so small
I am born of a wound.

I am born on the Feast of St. Monica,
the sun at high noon.
I dream young of Saviour's slender arms.
I weep a prayer.

Morning with the Son.
Light through the stained glass.
The scars on his wrists
like candlewax.
I trace them with my glove.

Outside my window,
women kneel.
They harvest tomatoes.
Flesh bleeds against their palms
and cast-iron pots.
September, and they stir their sauce.

Their mason jars
are open and clean.
Beautiful, for they bear
only light.

Bishop, you do not visit.
You are on your knees
making love to the Church.
You have never entered a girl.
You think that place is a wound.
Yes, a red hurt.

My father's madness pokes
under my door
like a dog's tongue.
He wakes me from sleep.
He is rabid tonight:
Wild and close as a sick coyote.
His legs are thin as crooked canes.

He sings me a song called
"Yellow Haired Woman"
though I am a girl.

His cigarette smoke rises
like signals from the Cree.
It wraps around my bedpost.
Vanishes through the stained ceiling –
like me.

His illness, its tributaries.
Outside, the river is a dark belt.
She is a dumb witness
and holds her tongue.

Daddy is uncouth.
His work boots stink.
He has not shaved.

In the morning,
he tugs at the earth
and harvests small fields.
He cradles new sheaves.

In the morning,
shadows of spirit-women.
I am made of flesh
and a soul so fine
he tore it in the dark.
It still bleeds.

But the women come,
the scent of healing salve
on their hands: Balm of Gilead.

Daddy takes coffee with cream and lithium.
Still, he doesn't shave during his manic phase.
I am so ashamed.

But I wax and wane too.
Today I am plum sad.
I took the Lord's name in vain:
"Jesus Christ," I cussed.
I must go on my knees like a penitent.

But it was Daddy who tore the family
like a photograph:
He and Mama and me
in our best cloth.

Yes, sickness grows in my mind
like an onion.
It pulls darkness inside its many skins.

I am weak as a kitten.
"Mama, take me by the scruff of my neck,
heave me in a burlap sack
where the river is wide."

Mama is a happy girl.
She has yellow curls.
The lowliest of things she loves.
Her heart a sacred bloody lump.
"We are made in the image of God," she says.
"The fullness of light and dark.
Nail the sickness to the cross."

Communion, but Daddy does not
take the host on his tongue.

He fastens stones to his shoes.
They sink like footprints on the ocean.

I write poems for Daddy
whose mind rusted like a little cage.

I limp to his funeral
on a dry winter day.
Wear velvet at my throat.
Sing hymns and pray.

I nurse a sick dog
with powders and pills.

Wash my body:
My hips and thighs.

Rouge my cheeks and lips,
line my eyes.

Tearful and lost
I wander the prairie.
My gown loose and torn.

I plant flowers
in the dry earth:
Lilies and lilacs, daisies and sage.

We live in a blue clapboard house now.
Mama drinks lots of milky steep.
And I make dreams.
I write them in a bound book,
a photo of my daddy pasted in.
We put him in a pecan box.
It cost lots.
But he does not come at night
or in the moments before sleep.

Zeus barks when Jesus stops by.
He brings me roses
for I was born a little sick:
My mind like a moon,
waxes and wanes.
Mama offers tablets
from a brown vial.
They are pink.
I take more when
it rains cats and dogs.

My belly is a begging bowl.
A prayer for soup, lumpy stew,
medicine, or crusty bread and cheese.
A pot of something warm.

In dreams, steam rises from my cup.
I think of a feather.
Tea brewed by Jesus.
His hand, a ghost, a vague white form.

I am an earthen vessel.
Mother dust on my knees.
Prayer at a miracle site.
Mary is a tent-dwelling woman.
When it rains her heart and the canvas beat.
Her summer frock is damp,
I imagine the shape of baby Jesus
pressed against her belly
like a fish into stone.
In the mornings,
I pace the prairie,
my bucket of fossils.

A flock of ghost-women.
Their hair dark
with the shine of feathers.
Their hearts fragile shells.

We rest by the shore:
A long sad caw.

My father's birthday.
I set a lily on his grave.

I rest then beneath my eiderdown.
My garment torn.

I bend to Jesus
for a little talk
beside my old iron bed.
Later, he pours out
a spirit of dream.
All night, my wheat fields weep.

In the morning, a loaf of bread
rises from my hands.
Outside, the autumn sun.
Shafts blow in the dust,
sacrifices in the wind.

Cool pearls at my throat.
I bend to the river
in my Sunday skirts.
Jesus falls upon me
like a shawl
and I do not shiver
in the cold.

I dance with Jesus:
A waltz with grace.
I wear new boots
and an Easter hat.
It snows this April,
though a lily opens
her torn lips to chant.

I wipe a tear
like a petal
from my wilted face.
But Jesus is an old root.
He takes deep root.
In his womb the calla lilies
bloom their Easter grace.

All day I harvest
and my hands bleed.
The flax is blue.

Then sleep blossoms from me.
My garment of gauze
is a swatch of light
like the moon.
I dream about Jesus
and his wounds.

Then a hard flat moon.
I dream of candles.
My heart is a pool of slow wax.
Jesus is a flame.

Birds, their plainsong.
Mary also says some pretty words.
I admire her hat made of feathers.
Jesus, his halo of bone.

I walk the river with my little dog
and the late women of this town.
They blow into me like a prairie breeze
and speak the language of the land.
It is lean and the shade of canola and corn.

The women are tired
for they hauled water
and bore sons and daughters.

They tell me of two loves to come:
One will beat my heart like a drum.
A man of the cloth will empty himself:
There will be twins.

The women are sudden and gone
like the wind.

Autumn, goldenrod
the river thick with leaves.

My dog tugs.

I think of you, Benny, this evening.
Your hair long,
the shade of tea tree.

Winter: Seasons since your first tattoo.
A blue eagle quivers on your arm.
Our bodies shiver on the shore too.

Benny slow dances and presses his lips
to Lucille's neck.
She is Wanda and Charlie's girl,
slim in a little red dress.
Benny gives her a slow kiss.

I remember a two step
on that horsehair floor.
His ancestors moved too.
I liked the scent of their medicine
on my bust.

I leave the dance,
the lyrics of "Kentucky Rain"
pelting and damp as Benny lusts.

My pickup truck is blue.
The sun is an old soul.
He wears paint on his face
the shade of canola blooms.

I empty my hurt into Lake Grace.

For a moment, I drown myself
beneath the water but rise again
through a little door.
Jesus and his crowd on the shore.

My pain floats like a dead fish.

My pickup truck bears
roots and herbs.
At dusk it is a dusty foot.
I wash it clean.

I take off my muddy boots and hose
at Reverend Hart's portal.
I cross his threshold:
Barefoot and chilled.
He holds me
and strokes my wavy hair.

Outside, a new moon:
I resolve to care for him
and bear us a babe.

His wife passed
in the season of ripening fruit.
In my dreams, she rests now
in an orchard of fallen pears.
She is bruised,
jaundiced and blue.

There is a god
of dying flesh and autumn dew.
A god, too,
of fertile then pregnant moons.

Reverend Christopher Hart
your hands are steady.
Through them wine and bread
become Christ.

Ordained, your neck is bandaged.
I poke my tongue beneath your collar.

My breasts rise like loaves.

Apparitions breathe the shapes of winter:
Like hoarfrost on a pane.
I salve their red hands with balm
or nourish them with thick cream.
Like a missionary, I offer gloves
in the name of Christ.

My husband's tongue is a muscle.
He lifts the Gospel beneath the new moon:
It is knife and light. It enters my heart like a clean blade.
We worship the body of the son, though his heart waned:
A pale bloodless thing, risen.

My husband, his burlap bag of seed.

The sun crawls on his soft, bruised knees.
Perhaps he gives thanks to the wind,
the way it wipes his brow.

My man sows.
And I bear a bucket of water.
The earth opens her dry lips and receives.

My hands tremble with the weight of the sacrament.
Clumsy, I pour and bless my dusty feet.

My husband lifts a trout from the river.
Its body is blood and flesh.
It is given and torn like the Son.

The sun also dies slowly this evening
and will rise again.

It is the month of June,
my husband's tongue like a root
in the dark hole of my mouth.
My heart a bloom.
Tuesday night, we waltz
in the parish hall.

Imagine Jesus dances,
holds the sexton's broom.
Barefoot. White soles despite dust.
Small miracles at St. Michael's.

My heart a stone in winter.
I dream of warm bread
and Lent.

Morning, my husband's truck,
a black nag.
A mechanical beast slow on gasoline.

The Holy Ghost blows.
Our red hands remember Communion.
The host now a shadow.
Solstice tonight: The memory of light.

Pyjamas are curtains drawn against night.
Pious and on our knees
we burn a candle.

Christopher enters my body,
a dark hollow like the hole in a tree.
A place for something wild to nest
like a bird.
The hole is damp and quiet.
It speaks dumb creed.

Winter solstice.
A full-moon eclipse.

Outside, angels pace
like a pack of cow dogs.
Blood on their lips.

Morning, my great belly
shrouded in bed.
Husband lifts the white blanket:
A cloud shifts.

I give birth
then bathe in pomegranate and fig.
A bar of soap wanes in my fist.
I imagine the lines on new hands
form constellations.

My belly was a Christmas bloom.
It waxed like the moon.

My water broke, a winter brook.
The twins swam from me.

I am a slim figure now
like a bare tree.

Babes, you are on my nipples.
My milk pale and given for you.

Christmas, my husband tears flesh from the bird.
A knife steady in his hand.
Bowls of warm potato, squash and turnip.

I nurse my children,
their soft mouths on my breasts.
My nipples little red blooms.

Outside, a cold winter rain.
The sun a memory.
The moon waxes like a woman
or Mary, her womb.

A minion of kind women wash my tired body:
Cool milk on a soft cloth.

They sing songs of children.

They shampoo my hair.
It is rooted in the first woman.
Damp now and long,
I tie it with a stem.

I lead the next hymn.
The women join me
in a harmony of Amen.

Twins: A girl named Martha
a boy called Simon.
I bathe them in warm waters
and gentle soaps.
They smell like heaven.

In a womb of time
the midwives lay
their hands on my twins' damp heads.
They will bury the placenta
in the herb garden.
Its fine hairs will sprout
from the earth's skin.

We pull Mother
on a sled through spring fields.
Some men break the virgin prairie
and make a hole there.
They lay her down.
The breeze is solemn,
does not love us gentle in his arms.
We kneel then stand
then kneel again.

I bury my mama by the river
in the soft belly of the earth.
Kind women gather
and pat the mound:
Warm in the spring rain.

All night I touch you, Love:
The white moons of your eyelids,
the horizon of your lips.
My hands are rooted in another life.
They bloom and fade and bloom.

My mama, too,
is a blossom:
Her new heart pale then red
as a fruit.

I think of her now
as I make love to you.
I turned in her womb
in an autumn morn:
A new life,
though apples rouged
and fermented in the ground.

I ride a dark horse
to the cemetery.
I pray the earth remembers she is Mother.
Her hair was thin as rain
and her heart was wild as weather.

Husband, bring your light.
I am dim today.

Fill my empty cornucopia.

It is autumn and death is upon me:
The slow blood, the fallen fruit
and the ghost of sun.

Tonight, the rains.
Hold me in the damp.
For I am without dog or Mama.
And the ache
is rheumatism in the heart.

My moon blood again.
I am balanced on the lap
of a witness tree.

Our daughter passed on the black moon.
She is cradled in the hips of the prairie.

My daughter is in a little box
lined in pink silk.
I pray an angel offers
her ripe breast
moist with sweet milk.

In the tug and blood of spring,
I grieve.
My mind is a dark moon.
The water is green.

Nurse roots through my sack.
Locks jars, creams and powders
in a metal cupboard.
I am bare faced as a child.

Roommate cries at night.
I bring her tea and a telephone,
the cord long as a root.

I eat my meals in bed:
A tuna sandwich and a piece of soft cake.
Spirit-dog rests at my feet.

Nurse is Cree.
She brings medicine in a paper cup.
I tell her, "I want to paint my face."

Daughter, my thoughts are quick fish.
A train moans.
Green waters quiver.

Later, at the Blackbird Café
I remember your hair:
Dark with the shine of feathers.

My husband, Reverend Christopher Hart,
so gentle and mild
did not wake this morning,
though it is Sunday
and he is to lead his small church
in the love of Christ.

His face is hard now,
though it was soft to my touch.

I will cover his lovely body
and drive him to town.

The spirits sing a sad tune.
I rub my aging womb.
The winter wind beats
against our little house.
I shiver in my nightgown.

My belly growls
like an old dog.
I stroke her.
She whimpers.
I pray the Lord
fastens a heavy stone to my foot.
For I am heart sick:
My gut is a bag of shifting bones.

My husband is a spirit.
His face is lace on the glass.

Our son, Simon, is wed this evening.
How handsome our lad.
And his bride, lovely in her tulle and dress.
They light the dim.

In the dream,
my husband balances a teaspoon
of water on my brow.
For there was original sin on my soul.
I move on him
praying to the moon.
The way it tears at the seam.
I am great with child.

In the morning, I am old again
and my womb is a broken clock.
Menopause: I do not wax and wane
or bear the shadow of Mother Eve:
All that blood.
Perhaps I am saved.

Mary and Jesus also sleep.
I dream they dream of me.

Biography

April Bulmer is a Canadian poet. She was born and raised in Toronto but has visited Saskatchewan where *Good Grief* is set. April holds Master's degrees in creative writing, religion and theological studies from major universities. Much of her writing deals with women and spirituality and the divine feminine. Many of her dozen books have been shortlisted for awards, including the International Beverly Prize for Literature in London, England, the Pat Lowther Memorial Award for the best book of poetry by a Canadian woman, the Next Generation Indie Book Awards in the U.S and the Global Book Awards. She won the YWCA Women of Distinction Award in the art and culture category in Cambridge, Ontario where she lives. Her work has also been celebrated and published widely in prestigious journals, anthologies and newspapers. For critical response to April's writing and more biographical information, please see www.aprilbulmer.wordpress.com. To purchase her books, please see www.aprilbulmer.com.

www.ingramcontent.com/pod-product-compliance
Lightning Source LLC
Chambersburg PA
CBHW022110160426
43198CB00008B/422